Leading
The
Curve

Maximize the efficiency, productivity, and adaptability of your business

Zechariah Blanchard

Leading The Curve

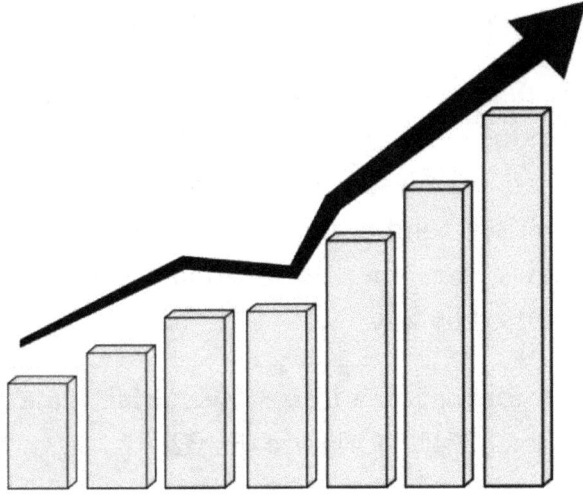

By: Zechariah Blanchard

I would like to dedicate this book to all leaders who fight to stay ahead of the curve. Civilization would be lost without them.

I would also like to thank my wife and two children. We could never spend enough time together. I love you guys more than life itself.

Table of Contents

Preface

I've been fascinated with leadership and human potential for as long as I can remember. It's inspiring to watch people come together in groups – large and small – to accomplish feats a single person could never do alone. And, the power of this community is placed in the hands of one leader. But, how do they lead their followers down the right path?

The more we learn about the human brain and how people react to outside actions, the more we learn about leading. The reason common practice in business has evolved over the years is because of new information constantly coming to the attention of leaders. Adaptation leads to an edge, and in business, an edge is everything. Still, the information won't come knocking on your door. If you want to learn the best new way to lead, you have to take advantage of available information. You, too, can be an organizational leader that's leading the curve and pushing the boundary of your industry.

Because of my love for advancement, I've engulfed myself in leadership books, videos, articles, and more. My passion led to a Bachelors of Science in Business Management from the University of Central Florida. Then I went on to continue my studies in the real world where I wrote my first book: <u>Creativity, Innovation, and Entrepreneurship: Keys to the Future of Human Society</u>. Now, more than ever, I see a need for quality leaders. Society has been crumbling under misguided leadership while entrepreneurs are using what science and research show us works to blow open the flood-gates of growth and profit.

You know, I've become accustomed to reading long, technical, and scope limited books about leadership, business, and entrepreneurship, but what I believe we really need in the leadership section of the bookstore is a book written about the many different practices utilized by the current market leaders. We need a book that offers its' readers a plethora of ideas to build up their team and grow market share. This book should be an easy read, give the reader a lot of information, and be written in a conversational tone. That's what I set out for in <u>Leading The Curve</u>.

Leaders and managers from all levels of organizations can learn a lot from the leaders and managers of other organizations.

Introduction

This ever-changing world we live in grows more competitive by the day. Survival in a shifting environment like ours requires constant adaptation. You can't survive without some kind of edge. And this edge comes from things like rapid adaptability, guided leadership, and consistency. Getting there takes a little elbow grease and know-how.

The survival of anything in a changing environment requires adaptation. Your organization must be able to shift with the markets. When your customers want something new, you need to have it waiting for them. The only way to accomplish this type of leadership is through a diversity of ideas. You will learn that these ideas present themselves when you know your people and have the ability to communicate with them effectively.

It doesn't stop there, though. Leaders need to know and understand their subordinates. The more you know and understand your people, the easier it is to effectively lead them to victory; one thing leads to another in leadership. We all want victory, don't we? This is something you can do right now to start leading your market. It doesn't always happen overnight, but true leaders get the most out of their people while leading them to victory.

Imagine an organization that works like a well-oiled machine. The company might lead the industry for overall sales and profit. But, what did they do to get on top? They utilized the known principles of management, leadership, and business, and it helped them succeed. It always comes down to what and who you know. What you know is all about the latest techniques. Who you know is where you utilize those techniques. Well-oiled machines have both.

The marathon to stay ahead of the curve is never ending, but there are things you can do to make it easier and more automated. Things like mentorships and succession plans will develop your people and provide you with another diverse body of ideas to utilize for making decisions on the edge of the curve. It is up to you to keep yourself educated on the best leadership practices. The fate of humanity lies in the hands of our leaders.

In this book, I have done my best to provide you with the information you need to begin leading the curve. Still, this information will do absolutely nothing for you if you never put any of it to use. We can only become better leaders through practice. This book is a blueprint. And, like most blueprints, it won't do anything for you if you don't take the time to read it and act on what it says.

Don't wait: Start reading your way into the leadership position of your industry now!

Image: Lead by Example

There is an old phrase I remember from childhood, "Do as I say and not as I do." Quality leaders don't hold their followers to a higher standard than themselves. Good leaders are the ones who say, "Follow my lead" and "do as I do." If you want to be out in front of the curve, be prepared to lead by example; all eyes will be on you and what you do. Because the entire company will be basing their decisions off the choices you make, lead by example and you can make your decisions count exponentially.

Life in the fishbowl comes at a cost. As the leader of your team or department, it is up to you to show everyone how they should be acting in - and outside of - the office. If you are coming in late, don't expect the employees to arrive early. If you wear tennis shoes to work, don't ask your people to wear dress shoes. Whether you like it or not, you are setting the example.

Consider your emotional state during a "fight or flight" event. These moments can easily catch you off guard. The adrenaline that pumps into your veins in these situations leaves you at a disadvantage. Lead by example and keep a calm demeanor during tense situations. The chance of a positive outcome will be greatly improved if you diffuse the situation instead of adding excitement.

Leading by example also includes the overall appearance of your position. You may be the manager of a multi-million dollar company and don't think it is a good idea to wear blue jeans to work. In some cases it's not appropriate, but in other cases it can be imperative.

The CEOs of some of the largest tech companies in the world wear jeans to work. Some of them don't even wear a button up shirt. It really depends on the image the job calls for. You need to have a presence that commands respect so people will follow you. Wear clothing that signifies the job and position. The president of a multinational corporation probably wouldn't dress the same as a construction site foreman.

Don't Get Complacent

Once you have taken the time to put some of the practices taught in this book in place, there will be a tendency to get comfortable and pay less attention to what is happening around you. Leading the curve requires a constant eye on the prize. You can never get complacent or your will lose your market position. It doesn't take long for someone to get ahead of your team.

While it *is* important to trust your people to do their job, it's imperative you keep a watchful eye and verify what is getting done. Keep a steady lookout to make sure your people stay sharp and don't become complacent. It doesn't take very long for employees and projects to veer off course, leaving their tasks in jeopardy of not getting done on time, or at all.

These things can cost the company considerable money. Sometimes this comes in the form of major project mistakes. These mistakes can easily throw a project so far off track that it never gets completed. The total cost depends on how much money is tied up in the project, department, or company. No matter, keeping a watchful eye on your people and verifying their work is an important step toward consistency.

Keep a dated log showing each time you speak to one of your employees and how often you give them an award or recognition. Make an award schedule and stick to it. Consistency is imperative. Give these awards out at least once a month (preferably at the moment they earn it). Each company is different, so you are going to have to decide how often to give awards to your people.

You can start enjoying a little relaxation once things are going smooth, but the more you relax, the further behind you will be when you get back to the grindstone. Walk your area on a daily basis and pick a few people to stop and talk with. Find out how they are doing and what they think could be done to better make the company more efficient. Always remember, you're leading by example; If you get complacent, so will your people.

Find Common Ground

Whenever you find yourself in a leadership role, do your best to find common ground with your subordinates. It's very hard to guide your people to success if you can't communicate with them. If you are perceptive, you can find common ground that allows everyone to relate.

Perhaps you wonder what kind of common ground I'm talking about. That isn't too hard to figure out. What things are going to benefit the both of you? There is always something you can use to connect with and better manage your people.

The common ground you are seeking may have even been in your face the entire time. All of the people in your department – including yourself – probably work in the same physical location. There are bound to be lots of things you have all dealt with at one point or another. Presumably, you experience the same traffic and weather patterns, eat the same kind of food, live in the same type of housing, and suffer the same local economic conditions. Every little thing you share in common is a potential access point for common ground.

This is extremely important in communication, too. Leading the curve requires you to communicate with your people effectively. The best way to do this is common ground because it relates directly to them. Don't forget, they are going to follow your lead and treat others the way you tear them. Find common ground and lead the way to a well oiled machine.

When you find your common ground it will help you connect with and manage your employees.

Attitude

The attitude you bring to work is going to resonate throughout the entire department. If you come in happy, the office will be happy. If you show up to work angry, everyone is going to have a bad day. If you come to the office too tired to work, it not only sends the wrong message, but people will use it as an excuse to slack off. Leading the curve requires a positive and consistent can-do attitude.

The attitude of the boss *and* employees is important, so always bring the best possible attitude with you to work. It will rub off on those under your leadership. If you work in a sales environment this should be a can-do-sales attitude. Your people need you to be the leadership super hero. That's your job.

Make sure when you come to work there is nothing but positive influences. Years back, I was working a management job I didn't enjoy. I arrived at work at 4:30am tired, joints hurting from the day before, no coffee, and shivering because of the weather outside. The last thing I wanted to do was get out of the truck and go into work, but I put a smile on and went in like I was happy to be there. I did it because there was no other acceptable option.

People depended on me to be there and get the job done. My attitude was what really mattered. I was there, sure, but my attitude would define the day for a lot of people. So, I told myself in the car, repeatedly, it was going to be a good day. Things were going to be positive. Everyone was going to get a lot accomplished.

This method I used of psyching myself up before work is a proven technique. Just the act of saying something like, "Today is going to be a great day" can drastically improve your outcome for the day. I don't know if anyone has ever noticed when I was not "happy" to be at work, but they never mentioned it if they did.

Energize Your People

The manager or leader is also responsible for energizing the workforce. When people are energized they become extremely aware of their surroundings. You might want to have an energizing speech before a big event. You can do this with a story or an inspiring speech. Either way, energizing people is extremely important in the modern age.

Employees are often so busy trying to keep up with what's going on, they lose sight of the energized work ethic. They sometimes appear run-down or dazed. Some call this "a case of the" "Mondays" or "Fridays." The lack of motivation damages productivity. These are perfect days to work on teambuilding. Getting people moving and working together will increase their energy and output.

Keep people enthusiastic about their job and they will work faster and more efficiently. If you have already given the entire department an uplifting discussion, but one person doesn't seem to have jumped on board, it just might take an individual conversation to energize them. This is a great opportunity to spend one-on-one time with an employee and get to know him or her better.

When you need to energize or motivate a small group or single employee, consider inviting them out to lunch or to join you on a short business trip. This will give you one-on-one time to figure out how to motivate them. Utilize this time to ask them questions about what they do outside of work. It is easier to motivate them when you know what they get excited about. Winning over a naysayer is a great way to win everyone else because they will take their enthusiasm and share it around the office.

If you try repeatedly and can't get someone on board, it might be time for them to consider other employment options.

Contagious Can-Do

Spread the can-do mentality around your department like a virus by creating and nurturing an environment that rewards positive risk-taking. If you punish failure without taking into account why someone failed it will degrade the can-do attitude of your entire company. Being held accountable for failure – even when it is intelligent risk taking that led to the failure – is an incentive to avoid risks. You can use the "can-do attitude" to get and keep your people energized.

Publicly rewarding people who take well educated chances will help you develop a supportive environment for creativity and forward change. You also have the option of rewarding those that try and fail. The trick is to remember not to promote failure, but the act of taking an educated risk. You can help this attitude catch on with those under your management.

With passing time, people will notice the rewards being given to those who try. They will begin to see the positive side of taking the right risks. This is the kind of behavior we want to promote as much as possible. It will get employees watching for ways to save money and increase efficiency. Let your people know they are always welcome to come speak with you about any idea to advance the department, people, or company.

Consider giving out an award every month to the person who took the most beneficial risk. You might think about adding a few different levels of award. These awards will further solidify the can-do attitude in your people. It's virtually impossible to get ahead of the curve without the ability to motivate your people. Find out what thrills them and use it to get your people excited about work.

Time Management

When it comes to time management, there are many different aspects one must consider. Mastery of time management requires practice. It's imperative you begin charting important future events. This gives you a look into the future so you can prepare when something is coming. Now, when a project falls behind, you are able to give extra attention to it and get it caught up.

I like to use a highlighter to make important events stand out. If you have a company executive coming, it might be a good time to highlight in red. I chose highlighter colors depending on the importance of the event.

Write yourself a to-do list with anything you need to get done. After you've finished writing the list, go down it and label things from most to least important. There are always going to be things you can and can't live without. You'll never have enough time to accomplish everything. Putting them in order will allow you to prioritize the most influential tasks.

Keep the most important things at the top of the list. Focus on accomplishing these harder tasks at the beginning, first. Completing a challenging task early in the day sets you on course for a day full of fulfilled jobs. Save the easier and less important things on the list for last. That way, if you happen to miss getting one done, it will be one of the least important.

Consider setting aside a specific chunk of scheduled time during the day to answer email and voicemail. Giving yourself enough time to answer them during a scheduled period frees up the remainder of your time to focus on the other tasks at hand. Maybe voicemail and email are low on your list and will be the one thing that gets pushed off for another day. The tasks that never get completed should be delegated to others.

There are many other things you can do to better manage your time. For instance, I like to ride public transportation, when it's available. This gives me the chance to catch up on a lot of missed reading. It also works to do the same thing on long trips. If there is another member of the group that can drive, it gives you time to catch up on things that might be of other importance. Proper time management is imperative to getting your team in front of the curve.

Delegation

Leading by example doesn't mean trying to do everything on your own. You need to utilize the people you have at your disposal if you want to become efficient. Take time to learn what everyone knows how to do and what they specialize in. This gives you an advantage in determining what you should and should not delegate.

Complicated and highly specialized tasks may require more than one person to work together to complete. Some of these tasks will require your assistance for completion, giving you an opportunity to teach people how to make smart decisions that help the company grow. The important thing is to remember the goal: delegation of tasks to people under your management because you can't do everything.

Great managers know that by themselves they can't accomplish half of what their employees can as a team. So, they focus on hiring the right people and letting them get the job done. If your people are not the right people for the job, maybe you need to consider retraining or helping them find a more suitable position.

After you delegate a task out, remember to follow up. Failure to check back with your employees about a task you assign them will leave you in the dark about whether the task was completed properly, or at all. You can't help your people and your business grow if you don't pay attention to what has been getting done. Businesses that lead the curve do an excellent job delegating to their people.

This is also a great opportunity to help your people learn a specialization. If you realize one person is extremely qualified to do a particular task, consider assigning them the responsibility of ensuring it is always completed. This can help build them up as individuals and also increase their total output as employees. Proper delegation practices can develop your employees, lower stress, free up leadership time, and diversifies your eyes on the ground.

Delegation is certainly a trait of curve leaders.

Success Plan

The success plan is an invaluable collection of research and decision making processes. This plan is very similar to a business plan. It should be extremely specific about what direction the business is going. At a minimum, the plan should include the development of key employees, strengths and weaknesses of the company, budgets, and growth strategy.

Never leave a key position in the hands of just one person. Success plans should include cross-training to cover important areas of business. You never know when a key individual will get sick or have to take an emergency leave of absence. Don't leave yourself at a disadvantage trying to train someone in the heat of the moment; make succession planning part of your strategic plan.

It's very hard to lead without a plan.

Strengths and weaknesses can make or break a company. Most people are more than happy to discuss their strengths, but cringe when their weaknesses are brought up. Get over this right away and spend time focusing on the weaknesses of the business, but don't let them get you or your people down. Knowing your weakness is imperative to fixing it, but don't let knowing destroy what you're creating.

I like to bring my team in for a group meeting and discuss the strengths and weaknesses of our unit. I make sure no question or answer is met with adversity. The purpose of this exercise is to show everyone where we can do better and where we have an advantage.

The success plan should include information about the budget. If you recently took your position, you may have to dig around for a copy of the old one. No matter, it is important to look at the budget over the past years and figure out where the money goes, why, and how to become more financially efficient. The flow of money in and out determines the overall success of a business. Know where you should and shouldn't spend money.

The last thing I like to make sure I have in any plan is a growth strategy. Great managers know who they are going to move up in the ranks as the company grows and people leave for other positions. Because you should never stop developing your people, this will be an ongoing matter. Your turnover rate shouldn't be from unsatisfied employees, it should be done to move onto a more prestigious position.

Build Yourself and Your People up

Managers that are not constantly building their people up are doing a disservice to themselves, their employees, and the company they work for. Promotion and advancement plans for your employees are imperative. You have a great chance to speak with your people about their development when you bring them in for a one-on-one meeting. Don't waste it. Use the time to find out their goals and aspirations.

Take the time to work out a growth strategy with them. Perhaps, depending on the type of job they are seeking, you are able to offer them some advanced training. Several times a year, leading companies send key individuals to training seminars. Some companies pay college tuition for employees. No matter the type of training you offer, it's important to constantly build up your people.

Shadow training days are a great way for employees to learn the job they may someday move into. Think of this like a take your co-worker to work day. Shadow training is where one employee trains another to accomplish the duties of their position. After the trainee learns the new job duties, consider scheduling them time in that position to keep the duties fresh in their mind.

You can accomplish a lot of this training through the setup of a mentorship program.

Start by putting your up-and-coming employees into it so they are better prepared for advancement into other positions. Over time, this will help you train people to fill the most vital roles. If you incorporate a mentorship training program you won't be left scrambling in the event of an emergency.

Vision

The success plan also helps you provide your people with a vision to work toward. Make sure your vision helps your employees understand the purpose of their jobs. The vision should show your people what the business will look like in the future. Leaders without vision leave their companies operating day to day. This lowers moral and drags down the amount of work being accomplished.

The people that work under you should understand the vision you have. You don't have to make it complicated. It doesn't need to be memorized by all the employees or even yourself. It's just a guiding hand to help people make decisions when there isn't anyone around to ask. The vision should help people understand the core reason for the existence of the business.

Here is an example vision for a fictitious pet store:

We provide customer service that creates super happy customers who go out and tell everyone about our stellar service. Our animals are all healthy and happy. No-one leaves our store without their guaranteed satisfaction. We have empowered employees to help our customers, so we never have someone leave unhappy.

In truth, it is virtually impossible to make everyone happy.

You don't have control over their attitude, but by giving them a look into why you make decisions, you can help them fulfill their duties without you around. So, ensure your people know what the general vision is for the company. Explaining the vision at a group meeting is a good way to get everyone on board. Strong visions show everyone you know how to get the company to the front of the curve.

Problems and Solutions

Problems and solutions can be found in business and in personal life. Because there are no problems without solutions, I like to ask the person bringing a problem to my attention for their solution. This works in many different ways. On one hand, there *is* a solution for every problem, but on the other, employees don't just offer them up. You've got to draw the solutions out.

So, every problem has a solution whether we have thought it up yet or not. It might not be easy to figure the solution out, but there is one. Even the wildest solution is still a solution. Don't permit people to bring you problems without solutions. All they succeed in when they do is stealing valuable time away from you. If they've noticed the problem, chances are they've thought about ways to solve it. As a curve leader, you need to draw the solution out of people.

Instituting a "Problems don't come without solutions" policy ensures more visits to your office will include a way to make things work better. You might even come across some great money savers and efficiency generators. Employees are the best solution creators at your disposal. If you happen to run across a problem without a quality solution, bring it up in the next meeting and get the opinion of your people. That's how curve leaders solve problems.

Effective Communication

Effective communication involves a lot more than just saying something and having someone else hear what you've said. Communication has a myriad of different noises that get in the way of effective communication. You need to communicate in a way the recipient will understand. Sometimes, just the tone in your voice is enough to completely change the meaning of your message.

Earlier, we discussed finding common ground with the people you work with. This common ground is what you use to effectively communicate with your employees. Understanding how someone thinks or feels is important in ensuring you get the right message across. Ineffective communication is like sending a message to someone in a foreign language and expecting them to interpret it properly.

Environment can have a dramatic impact on how well your communication works. The simple act of holding a meeting in your office is a powerful move that puts the other person on the defensive. Meeting with an employee in their place of work can help level the playing field. Where you hold the conversation should depend on what you need to accomplish.

Listening is a giant part of communication. Focus on understanding the group you need to communicate with and your conversations will begin to flow naturally. Every situation is different, but when I can, I listen more than I speak. Good listening and topic direction is one of the best forms of communication I have used with employees.

Remember to use the methods and words they would use in communication. If you don't already know what words and gestures they use, spend some time around the office with your people and find out. Listen for the tone of voice when they speak. What is the energy level? What are they discussing? These will all help you in your quest for effective communication. Leading the curve requires an effective communicator.

Methods to Communicate

You will be spending a lot of time with your people. Use this time to figure out what methods they use to communicate. This can be an easy exercise or a hard one. It really depends on your background, education, and other life experiences. Not to mention, there are more methods of communication out there than language. Attitude, body language, tone of voice, location for conversation, position in the room, clothing type and color, and many other factors can influence the message. Effective leaders make sure their communication is being received correctly.

You may find the people in the office go out to a restaurant everyday for lunch. This is a great time to join in and learn how to better communicate with them. Find things you both have interest in and use it to lay the groundwork for clear communication. Actively listen to the group while you are eating lunch and take note of the things they talk about and the word choices they make.

I find using analogies with people is extremely effective. Not everyone is good at communicating with analogies at first, but in time you will get better. They can be used to explain almost anything. A decent analogy is like a great picture – clear and worth a thousand words. Usually, they are so basic that anyone can understand them.

Open and Ongoing Communication

Managers that lead the curve maintain an "Open Door" policy. This doesn't mean the door is physically open, but it means anyone in the company can talk to the boss. These leaders are willing to find or make the time for their people. Open door policies help keep leaders informed of what is going on in their business. Everyone who aspires to be a better leader should institute an open door policy.

Maintain an ongoing and open communication structure in your office to build relationships. After a few months you will begin to see the return in teamwork, productivity, and efficiency. You need to spend time speaking to your employees on an individual level. Constantly communicating with your people will help you better prepare for random occurrences.

Without ongoing communication you wouldn't know Mary is having a baby until she puts the paperwork in with HR to take her maternity leave. That could leave you in a rough spot if Mary is responsible for a large project. This is all part of the employee development strategy and success plan. Through the utilization of an ongoing communication program, your people and you will rarely, if ever, be left scrambling to get unforeseen things done before a deadline. Market leaders work constantly to communicate with their people.

Clear and Specific Goals/Expectations

While working with people on their goals and expectations, it is important to keep them involved, and to ensure you are very precise in the requirements. The more room for interpretation in goals and expectations, the more likely people are to utilize the obscurity to make up their own specifics – right or wrong. Giving your people clear and specific goals will help them become more productive for themselves and the business.

Have each employee help you write out the goals and expectations for themselves. They are the most qualified person to interpret and write what is required of them. No one can communicate with them like they can. Just make sure the goals and expectations are clear and specific. Your job is to direct what is required and allow them to word it in a way they understand best.

You don't want a goal like, "Become manager" because it isn't clear and specific enough. Think more along the lines of, "Become the manager of a branch office, in Jupiter, Florida, with 10 or more employees, making a six figure income, within the next two years." Clear and specific solidifies exactly what is to be accomplished.

Expectations should always target some kind of measurable outcome. When setting them, aim for a numerical figure that can be used to measure against what actually happens. Sally needs "$12,000.00 worth of total sales for the 2014 year before Friday (February 13, 2014)" in place of "Sally needs to improve sales figures." One is clear and specific, the other is not.

Carefully define the objectives of goals and expectation so they can't be misconstrued. Help your employees write goals and expectations in their own words. Just guide them in what they write. Make it a friendly environment by doing it in their place of work instead of your office. Following the rule of "clear and specific goals and expectations" will help you and your team move ahead of the curve.

Consistency

Management is a type of celebrity; albeit one we might not want. Still, we are constantly in the spotlight as leaders. Employees notice every mistake and use them to defend their own actions when they break the rules. Be consistent. "Do as I say and not as I do" is not an option for managers leading the curve.

If you aren't consistent, your employees won't be consistent. They will walk the walk when you are looking, but if you don't follow your own rules, behind your back, neither will they.

It's not only important for you to consistently follow your own rules and regulations; everyone must always be treated with the same consistent reprimands and rewards. Curve leaders are not lenient when it comes to rules and regulations.

Consistency means doing things the same, every time. When it comes to being late, either you excuse everyone, every time, or you excuse no one, ever. Everyone has to be held to the same standards. Consistency will pay off. Soon, everyone will know what you say goes and will be okay with it, but you must be consistent. People can plan around consistency.

All Around Accountability

Accountability creates predictable behavior. When people are held to a standard, and are accountable to that standard, they tend to consistently perform better. It's harder to forget what you are working toward when it is "written in stone" as they say. Accountability goes for individuals as well as management.

You need to hold yourself to as high (higher is better) a standard as everyone else.

When you are consistent with people, they know they are held to the same standard as everyone else. Combine this with accountability and documentation and you have a workforce holding themselves accountable. The main person they don't want to let down is themselves. To lead the curve, hold them accountable for their actions, goals, and expectations.

Step Outside Before You Decide

Sometimes in leadership we find ourselves in a position we really don't want to be in. Perhaps one of our employees is having an extremely bad day at work and has been acting irritated. You might have gone over to remedy the situation, but found the employee was rash with you, too.

So, you approached them and they were out of line. You might not want to reprimand them right now because it could escalate the situation, so you go outside (or to another room) and spend a few minutes considering what led to the action and how to proceed. All it takes to lead the cure is five minutes away from the situation. Five minutes to think about it objectively.

We often overreact in the heat of the moment. What could just be a simple mistake by a quality employee ends up costing them their job. Consider the gravity of the situation before you decide what punishment – if any – is necessary. You might save yourself a lot of headache finding a replacement for someone that shouldn't be leaving anyway.

Sometimes it is better to give a little in a situation than to escalate it to a point of no return. You don't always lose face by giving in to someone. It can be seen as an act of kindness as long as you never escalate the problem to begin with. Once it has taken off, you can't do near as much to stop it. If you don't want to hurt your chances of staying ahead of the curve, step outside before you decide. Five minutes is all it takes.

Obviously, if there is any physical danger of violence you want to contact the appropriate authorities.

Employee Happiness is a Good Thing

There are managers that don't believe employee happiness has anything to do with their bottom line. That couldn't be further from the truth. Be it sales, service, or manufacturing, happy employees work harder, produce more, and retain more of their experience for future challenges.

Inevitably, happier employees will lead to happier customers. In the eyes of the customer, service with a smile is better. Customers are more likely to walk away satisfied if they enjoy their conversation with your employee. Smiles and general happiness result in better quality ratings for your company. People like to be around happy people. They shop at places where the people make them feel good and special. This goes for whoever it is your business operates to serve.

Happy customers rave to people about you and send more business – or budget – your way. Either way, this is a win for the entire department. It only takes one person to change an entire organization. That person could very well be you. Keep smiling and infect others with happiness. Lead the road with happiness and others will surely follow.

Win/Win

Win/Win situations *can* exist if you are willing to look for them. These are the best solutions to any problem because both parties gain in a win/win. When your employees gain something they value, motivation increases. You can use this to the advantage of everybody. Always seek out a solution where all parties can walk away a winner. This doesn't just go for business. Don't underestimate the value of saving face in all aspects of life.

Not every situation can be a win/win, but most of them can. There even companies that have turned terminations into win/win situations. They help the employees being let go find employment elsewhere. This helps them avoid other costs associated with terminations. In turn, the employee gets a job as good or better, and the company is able to save money and become more efficient. Leading the curve requires repeat business and experienced employees. Win/win atmospheres promote the growth of both.

Work to make all situations win/win. You never know when a win/win today will have an even bigger payoff tomorrow.

Network Building

Business is, in a lot of ways, all about networking. Who you know and how well you know them can be a make or break. Even if you never do business with anyone outside your company, you are still networking. You need to take the time to network for your department inside and outside of the company. People who already have an extensive network are a great addition to yours.

If there is a print marketing emergency, you need to know who can get your materials printed and to you faster than anyone. Who on your list will come in to work early, or stay extra late to make sure you have the materials you need? These are the people you want to keep in touch with. Fill your network with other curve leaders and create a super network.

Your network should include people across the industry. Lot's of information can be shared across businesses within a market. Wholesalers are almost always happy to discuss new products and services with potential buyers. They can also be a great place to call on when you need a product super fast. Networking across the industry is extremely important. People do business with people they like, and they can't like you if they don't know you.

Networking outside of the company can get you, your company, and your people publicity and name recognition. This will increase sales and provide you with more stability for tough economic times. When your back is against a wall and the deadline is approaching, you will be happy you have an extensive network. There exist a multitude of places you can go to network.

Some of the places I like to network at include: wine tastings, local speaking clubs, business and political events, and chamber of commerce meetings. The most important thing is to network at places that make you comfortable. One of my old bosses networked best at car shows and another one was most successful at home shows. They loved talking about their craft and these were the best places for them to network with potential clients.

No matter how you decide to build your network, write down a little about each person and what they do for work. Store and review this information before you speak to them again. When your network becomes vast it is very hard to keep track of each person. Writing down just a little bit about a person can do a lot to jog your memory next time you meet.

Networking goes both ways. You may like being able to rely on your network, but don't forget your network also needs to rely on you. This is a two way street. When you hear of a job opening or new business venture someone in your network would like to hear about, call and inform them. Never let an opportunity slip through your hands. People will reward you for thinking about them. Good networking will keep you well informed of who is leading the curve. If you have the largest network in your industry, it will likely be you.

Keep a contact list for your network and send them an email once in a while. I have used mail services for this before. There are even some good free ones available. Search for "free business email services" on your favorite search engine.

Know Your People

It is hard to delegate and communicate like an industry leader without knowing your people. Get to know them each personally. Have a private meeting with them. Choose a neutral area like the break room. This is a great exercise when you first start working at a new job. Let them get to know you, too, by encouraging them to ask questions.

This is a great time to find out - and record - what type of reward each person likes. Rewards are much better when we are given what we want. Not everyone enjoys being given an award in front of the group. It might even be a negative incentive if you do that with the wrong person. Some people get extremely nervous when in front of their peers. Make sure you ask before you assume.

You may also want to discuss the direction they want to take their career. Help set them on a path of growth and development. The easiest way to do this is to work on a career development plan with them. This is quite the challenge because a lot of people don't even know what they want, but stick with it and everyone will be better off.

Help your subordinates grow their professional and personal lives. There are bound to be things in their personal life they want to accomplish. Working with them – to the extent acceptable in your work environment – to plan out and accomplish their personal goals can improve performance at work. Growth and development of those around you will almost always have a positive impact on your business.

Promote Your People

Never pass up a chance to market one of your people. An employee getting an award brings notoriety to your department and company. When one of your people does something worth talking about, take the time to let them know you noticed and reward them with the type of recognition they will appreciate. Others will be more likely to follow their lead when they can see you rewarding them for their efforts.

No matter who is responsible for getting a job or project completed, always shower your people with praise. I am not saying you should lie about what they did, but when you can, offer praise to your people. Building people up for doing good things and giving them the credit makes them work harder. It also solidifies your position as their leader. Respect for you will grow as you offer praise to others.

Send your people out to learn new things when the opportunity presents itself. Trade shows and other events are a great place to promote your business and people. Have your best and most knowledgeable employees spend time at trade shows. If the show is far away, just send two people to attend. These steps will help you grow your brand through growing your people. Promoting your brand and people keeps you leading the curve.

Mentorships

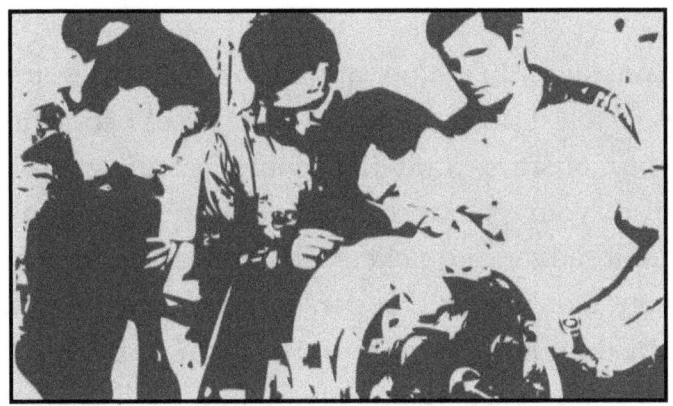

Mentors are important in anything you do, not just leadership in business. Having someone there for you - that has done what you are doing - is invaluable. It's like having the experience of doing something before, but you get it through another person. It offers a different perspective from someone who knows you; it's a look at the situation from the outside. This often leads to a better final decision.

Good mentors are people you respect. They are willing to devote time to helping you grow as an individual. Mentors should not expect anything in return for their services. Your personal mentor is probably someone leading the curve in their industry.

You shouldn't stop at finding a mentor for yourself. I'm certain there are a lot of people in your business unit that could benefit greatly from your guidance. Find someone you think could advance quicker with some insight from you. Don't offer this person special treatment, but do a little extra to move them in the right direction. Just make sure it doesn't look like special treatment. You don't want to do anything that might violate company guidelines.

You can also mentor friends' employees in exchange for the same in return for your people.

Encourage the person you mentor to go the extra mile and always give their best. Let them know you believe in them. It is up to you to become a mentor or find yourself a mentor. Mentorship is something that can only be done through a choice; there is no point in trying to force someone. Continue to perform the same business function you always have for your employees. Just because you have taken on the title of mentor doesn't mean you're done helping everyone else.

Finding Your Mentor

Your mentor should be someone that knows you and can help guide you in your industry. They should be a person you trust. Great mentors are individuals who have achieved the things you are looking to achieve. They have experience and network connections that can speed you along the way. You might even find a mentor in a close friend or boss. The right mentor can help you stay ahead of the competition.

There are so many places to look for a mentor. Small organizations exist just to connect people who have accomplished something with people looking to achieve great things. This might be a good place to check if you can't find someone you personally know. Also, consider attending one of these organizational events to find someone you can mentor. It is not always appropriate to mentor someone that works in your department.

Mentoring Others

Mentoring others requires you to take time out of your day and give back to the community that helped you get to where you are. No two mentoring situations are the same. Sometimes all that is needed is a little guidance and direction. Other times, mentors may have to make phone calls and take time out of there day to attend events. Mentoring is not a small job. It can be time intensive now and again.

Still, mentoring people is a great way to invest in the future. You get to help someone grow, develop, and thrive. Lead your people away from the pains and stress you experienced on your way up the corporate ladder. This is your time to help other people have it better than you ever did.

Key Influencers and Leaders

Every group of people has key influencers and leaders. These are the people others follow because they respect them. Key influencers are not always people with real organizational power. Anyone from the lowest employee to the top executive can be an organizational influencer. Usually, they are just like everyone else, only they've spent considerable time getting to know and making friends with everyone. If you want to stay ahead of your competition, you need to get these people on your side.

Spending the time to talk with key influencers about upcoming changes is like peering into the future. Their reaction to what you propose will likely be the reaction of the company as a whole. Working through any issues ahead of time to get leaders and influencers on board is a good way to ensure change happens without any hold ups.

Talk to your key influencers personally. Find out what they want out of the job. Information like this will help you grow them in the company to take the place of other leaders as they leave or transfer out. Influencers are good allies to have. Maximize your resources.

True Equality

We hear about equality all the time. There aren't many people who believe we should support inequality; just treat everyone the same. True equality means no matter what the individual characteristics of someone are, you judge them based on the content of their character and the quality of their work.

Gender, age, sexual orientation, and color should have nothing to do with business. The question you should be asking is what will make the business most likely to succeed? This question can only be answered when you consider the abilities of each employee and forget about the characteristics of their physical conditions.

There are always going to be times when you need to consider some other traits. It is okay to do this if these other traits are a requirement of the job. You should have the requirements spelled out in the job description. When they are clear, specific, and laid out in a job description, it should be impossible for anyone that can't do the job to get the job.

Ensure people are all treated the same in your place of business. Never let employees make each other feel singled out or harassed. Treating someone different based on minority - or other – traits is wrong and will cause the business a lot of trouble down the road. Take part in the great diversity humanity has to offer. You will get better results with a team of people from different backgrounds. The more viewpoints you have, the more likely you are to be leading the curve.

Diversity of experience, education, and upbringing is vital to a creative and adaptive business.

Adapt With Change

Adaptation to change is imperative. It may seem like a no brainer, but people ignore the danger of failing to adapt. The picture I chose for this chapter is of an old typewriter. This symbolizes the way things were once done - from book writing to business documents. Indeed, some people still use typewriters for nostalgic reasons (and there are probably at least a few people that refuse to upgrade to a computer, even today).

Now, imagine if we were still using old fashioned typewriters and printing presses for all of our printing needs. There is no way we could keep up with the speed at which the world moves today. Early adopters of the computer may have spent a lot of money on the computing power they had, but they also had an advantage over their competition. Eventually, the advantage got large enough to weed out companies who refused to adopt computers.

Without computer programs to encode and decipher what we write, there could never be e-books.

Those that chose to stick with typewriters and a slew of typists spent a considerable amount more on labor costs. Eventually, businesses changed over to computers or became obsolete. You don't know what the future is going to bring, but realizing when to change, and getting it done fast, is what industry leaders are remembered for. If you aren't willing to adapt to change and help others do the same, you are welcoming failure.

Change comes in many forms. Physical copies of documents are replaced with electronic ones. New social media platforms are born and old ones fade away. Customer bases and products change with time. Manufacturing standards change to adapt to overseas competition. We must learn how to spot and embrace positive change. Curve leaders adapt themselves so they can see when and where to change.

People shun change because it scares them. You should make change easier for your employees by taking time to discuss what is going to be different and why it needs to be changed. The better you communicate the message, the more your people will welcome the change. You have the ability to make change a positive movement instead of a problem.

Adapt or Become Obsolete

If you don't adapt to new economic conditions, someone else will. Then, they will slide in, take your job, and put your company out of business. It happens more often than you might want to believe. Disruptive entrepreneurs seek this kind of opportunity out; ripe industries allow newcomers to sweep in and take control of a significant portion of the market. One of the quickest ways to the front of the curve is to grow your share with a method your competition doesn't or can't utilize.

Leaders don't only have to be prepared to adapt to change, they need to be ready to help others adapt as well. The best way to do this is to fully understand the change being made, and use your understanding to explain to your subordinates how it's going to help them. You might discuss job security or company stability. Maybe you need to remind everyone that outsourcing has taken several jobs away already. Make sure you show the employees how the change is going to benefit them.

If you have a problem figuring out how the change will benefit the employees, talk to your mentor or upper management and get their opinion. They might be able to offer some type of guidance for your change management meeting. Some companies even hire in specialists to help with change management. The faster you learn to adapt, the easier it is for your organization to lead the curve.

Problem Solving

Problem solving can be done in a few simple steps. First, we need to identify the problem we are having. Then, you want to define the root cause. Once you know the root of the problem, you can start brainstorming fixes. Picking a solution and implementing it is next. Lastly, you will need to monitor the new solution.

Identify the problem. This seems relatively straightforward. Indeed, you can usually identify the problem you are having rather easily. The hard part comes in defining the root cause of the problem. The following example walks you through problem solving.

Problem: Gary is not completing his work on time.

Defining the root cause requires us to ask:

What exactly is stopping Gary from completing his work on time?

Cause: Gary is spending a lot of time outside on the phone, smoking cigarettes.

The time Gary is spending on the phone and smoking cigarettes might not be the actual root cause, though. Digging deeper, we find the root cause of the problem.

Root cause: Gary has a close family member who is sick in the hospital. His entire family is stressed out and they call him for support.

Now that we know what the problem is with Gary, we can start considering solutions. They may look like this:

Tell Gary he just can't make personal phone calls or have cigarette breaks during business hours.

Terminate Gary and replace him with someone new.

Hold a meeting in which you tell everyone what is going on with Gary and ask for their support.

Talk to Gary and recommend he take vacation time to be with family.

With several solutions now available, we need to pick the best one. The best choice from our example is probably, "Talk to Gary and recommend he take vacation time to be with family." So, call Gary into the office and have the discussion with him. It doesn't pay to be pushy or to hesitate. Make sure you use compassion when talking to someone in the same position as Gary.

Monitor the results of your plan. In this case, you will want to monitor Gary and his work when he returns from vacation. If he doesn't improve and is still on the phone and smoking a lot, you may consider a different course of action.

Overall, you are searching for solutions that last. Brainstorming several different solutions will help you find the best choice. It can take time to properly identify a problem. Write down what is happening and why. Dig down with questions until you get to the root of the problem. Once you find the root cause of the problem, brainstorm for solutions, implement them, and monitor the results. The best paid CEOs in the world are hired for their problem solving and decision making abilities.

Diversity

Diversity has been beaten into the heads of leaders for quite some time. I don't want to go into too much detail, but will explain why diversity is important to you and your business. Actually, diversity is important to society as a whole. Diversity is what has made America great for so long. Fostering diversity better prepares us for unknown future competition.

Competitive environments constantly evolve to weed out weak or outdated businesses. This is the evolution of business and products we often hear free market economists discussing. Basically, this drives business to compete until there isn't any profit left in the market segment. It's the "perfect" "free market economy" where – over time – the consumer becomes the biggest winner. This is why diversity is so important. To lead the curve, you need to stay ahead of market changes.

Be the business that comes up with new ideas faster than everyone else. Your business should represent the best of the best. Never settle for second fiddle. Diversity offers you the ability to make rapid decisions for advancement. A variety of backgrounds leads to a variety of ideas. These ideas help you solve problems and increase efficiency.

Diversify your business over time to add more variety to the ideas and products in your portfolio.

Fostering Diversity

It is not a bad idea to have a diversity plan. The diversity of ideas and products that come out of your company are probably directly related to the longevity of your job. Only through constant change can you stay on top, grow, and beat out the competition. If you are up against a diverse world of businesses, you need to diversify your possibilities, else you will become obsolete. With the speed of business today, obsolescence can come in the blink of an eye.

There are many ways you can begin to foster diversity. A good place to start is your hiring practices. If you are looking to diversify your business for competitive purposes, look for people that are outside your general employee pool. You want someone that will come in with a different opinion. It doesn't matter what quality sets them apart, you want someone that thinks different than the majority of your employees.

Whether holding a group event, a meeting, or a one-on-one training session with an employee, encourage people to ask questions that are outside of the box. Reward creative thinking and different points of view. Ask for opinions on upcoming changes to the business. Get people chiming in and encourage a plethora of ideas. You may be pleasantly surprised - at your options - when you find out how many ideas your employees keep to themselves.

Assign group projects. Group projects force people to work out the best course of action from a diverse list of ideas. It isn't the perfect environment (alpha people usually form inside groups), but it creates a team mentality. Once in a while, it's a good idea to change who is in a group. This shouldn't be mandatory unless it is needed.

Utilize and cherish the diversity in your workforce and you'll remain at the head of the curve.

Stress

It's no secret that stress is bad for you and your health. However, research does suggest a certain level of stress is beneficial to your health and productivity. But, I'm going to focus on stress reduction. Stress from leadership roles has a tendency to build up over time. It's important for you to be able to spot and manage this stress.

Getting to the cause of stress - and working to eliminate it - increases productivity and general health. Good stress management is imperative for those leading the curve.

Some of the ways to limit or lower stress are taking breaks, walking, healthy eating habits, regular exercise, and getting adequate sleep. Work to keep everyone in the office "in the know." Encourage employees to take breaks and walk around. Offer healthy snacks in the break room. Hold workshops on healthy eating and sleeping habits. Educate your people on stress and don't let stress get the best of you, either.

Make sure your employees take their vacation pay each year. The time away from the company can provide a full reboot or recharge for a vacationing employee.

Understand Your Limitations

Leaders from all levels have a hard time with their own limitations. We work extremely hard to get ahead and forget we can't do everything alone. There are always going to be specialties and specialists. We can't be everything for everyone. Knowing your limitations allows you to better manage your time and efficiency.

You may be extremely good at financial management decisions. Perhaps you are the best in the industry. You might even be the person who wrote the textbook. It doesn't matter how great you are at making financial management decisions, it doesn't make you particularly good at legal decisions, or decisions about operations, or even human resources decisions. In this case, one does not make you good at the other.

Know your limitations. Find someone to take care of the areas that would be better handled by a specialist. This could be accounting, human resources, general paperwork, phone calls, computers, or anything. Using the most efficient source for important tasks frees up your time to focus on other things. It also helps your company produce a product that's a cut above the rest.

Delegation is a great tool. When used properly, it will help secure your position as an industry leader.

Trust the Expertise of Your People

I had the opportunity to speak on-on-one with the CEO of a national truss company (years back) and asked him about his management philosophy. He told me, "I find the right people and get out of their way." I thought this was an interesting philosophy, so I asked for more information. Being an industry leader, he was more than willing to explain his reasoning for how he managed.

Basically, he told me quality managers find the right people for the job based on skill, experience, attitude, and other qualifications. Once they have the right people, they get out of their way and let them do the job they were hired for. If they have a problem, they are welcome to seek guidance. Your job isn't to micro-manage their actions, it's to help guide the general direction of the company. Trust the people you choose, verify what they do, and guide them when needed. Leading the curve requires you to be ahead of your competition. Make sure the best people for the job are the ones making the decisions for you.

Trusting your people can also increase efficiency within your business. People tend to accomplish more work under the right kind of indirect pressure. Stress levels go down when people can work at their own pace (so-to-speak). Also, when you trust your people, there is more time available for managing the other duties of your position. Research also suggests autonomy can reduce employee turnover, sick days, and personal days. Be a quality manager and trust your people to get the job done you hired them for.

Decision Making Skills

Teaching your people decision making skills is a great way to delegate work and mitigate stress. When one of your people has a question about how to proceed, work through the solution with them. Walking them through the solution process should give them a better understanding of why you make the decisions you make. Teaching other people increases your overall productivity.

Don't punish mistakes; encourage your employees to make decisions without you. Over time, as their confidence grows, you will see improved performance. This learning process can take time. You have to get through any initial onslaught of mistakes. Don't abandon the ship early. Curve leaders stick it out to the end for the potential they need to get out front.

It reminds me of a story I was told about a man who makes a huge mistake and costs his company a fortune. The man is understandably stressed out about the situation. The amount is more than double his annual salary. He was certain he would lose his job when his boss found out. But, he sucked it up and went to tell his boss.

Braced for termination, he stood in front of his superior and explained what happened. He didn't get fired, though. When he asked his boss why he still had a job, the boss replied, "I just spent a fortune training you what not to do. I'm not giving you up now. Your mistake was a learning experience I don't think you'll repeat. If I hire someone else without the same experience, they may make the same decision and cost me money again."

Some lessons in business cost more than others, but there is no reason to waste a costly mistake. If the responsible party learned from their mistake, and you don't think they will repeat the error, keep them on-board. You just spent a fortune training them. When you lead an industry, you have to savor anything that gives you an edge over the competition.

Public Speaking

Speaking in front of large groups of people doesn't come easy to most of us. Research shows public speaking is the number one fear of Americans. Most of the fear associated with public speaking is unfounded. We worry that everyone will make fun of us or we will sound stupid. Basically, we tend to build a mountain out of a mole hill. It won't get easier until you practice, practice, practice. You can't lead from the sidelines.

Repetition will make it easier for you to go out in front of groups without appearing nervous, but the butterflies will be there for a long time.

Whether you are running for public office, holding a meeting with your subordinates, or doing a presentation for your boss or customers, the more you speak, the better you get. Try to get yourself pumped up ahead of any public presentation. There are lots of little tricks to help with your nerve. Nothing will ever replace getting out and practicing, though.

Meetings

Holding meetings requires you to maintain the leadership position. This does not mean you have to do all the speaking (but it is a good idea to get the practice whenever possible). Bring a list of topics to discuss and be ready to take questions. Make copies of the list and pass them to the attendees so they have something to follow along during the meeting. Make it a point to hold at least one meeting a day. Some basic ground rules will make meetings easier to control.

Even though you can have department heads and team leaders do some of the speaking at your meetings, you should begin and maintain control of them. When it is time to call the meeting, start with chit-chat like, "How is everyone doing today!?" Ask if they are ready for a great day. Get them involved in the meeting so they will pay attention. If your meeting lasts longer than ten minutes, you will begin to lose the attention of your audience, but you can increase attention span by involving the audience in the meeting.

Preparing ahead of time with a list of topics to discuss will help your meetings run smooth and ensure you don't miss anything important. The meeting should cover past, present, and future news of the business. Write a quick document in some kind of word processing program, make copies, and give them out before the meeting. You can get creative with these, but try not to draw too much attention away from the topics of the meeting.

Hold regular meetings and make sure there are ground rules. Rules can make your meetings much more effective. Regular meetings keep everyone informed to what is new in the company, provide consistency, and give managers the opportunity to hear about problems directly from their people. Keeping communication streams up and running is extremely important to a healthy and productive work environment. Having general rules will ensure the meeting stays on topic and gets done in a timely manner.

It is hard to stay at the front of the curve if you don't get out there on a regular basis and have an open dialogue with your people.

Presentations

Sometimes you're speaking to such a large group of employees or co-workers you are actually doing a presentation. Presentations are run differently than meetings, but have the same basics: visual aids, agendas, rules, start and end times, and one person in charge of direction. Microphones help a great bit when you are in a very large room. Good presentations can shock and amaze people in your industry.

It is a good idea to use a projector or some other type of visual aid when presenting. Keep the amount of information on any presentation slides low. You want the crowd paying attention to you, not your visual aid. Try to limit yourself to a slide for every few minutes of speaking. This will help keep the group focused on you and provides you with a primitive timer.

Your slides should be a basic representation of your talking points. When you move through the slides, they will help you remember to talk about each topic. Slides can also offer your audience a quick look ahead. The last slide may be a way to contact you, a slide asking for questions, or just a "thank you" for inviting you to speak. Don't make your slides too distracting. You won't be reading them directly and you don't want them drawing attention away from your presentation.

Start and end times are an example of a general rule for your presentation. Your audience wants to know when they need to be in place and when they will be able to leave. It is up to you as the presenter to ensure you start on time, maintain order, and end on time. Don't forget to leave time at the end for questions. Taking questions from the group offers you the opportunity to become a better presenter and connect with your audience.

Toastmasters

There are great organizations out there geared toward helping people become better public speakers. The one I most often hear about is Toastmasters. Organizations like this offer you the chance to meet other professionals and work as a team to develop each others' speaking skills. Some of these events offer small prizes to people as they advance. These groups have stringent rules about being constructive with speakers and encouraging them to speak again. It's hard to lead the curve if you can't get out and speak in front of an audience.

Check for a group like Toastmasters in your area. You can improve your public speaking skills and network with other professionals at the same time.

Teamwork Development

Development of teamwork will make your department operate a lot smoother. Complicated jobs and tasks are simplified and completed more rapidly when people work together. It also gives you the opportunity to cross-train key people. When your employees start working together as a team, they start producing like a machine. Teamwork development is something leading organizations champion and so should you.

There are many ways to foster the growth of teamwork. Cross-training brings employees together that might otherwise never speak to each other, gives them another person to add to their network, and teaches them another job for emergency situations. If you want a more personal touch, consider game days. Group outings offer outdoor activities to your team. And, there are always group rituals to give everyone common ground. Don't forget to include your employees in deciding how to develop the group teamwork; they are a vast source of ideas and the stimulation couldn't hurt them.

Cross Training

Cross-training is a great way to develop teamwork and strengthen your business unit. This type of training strengthens your team and teaches them to fill more than one position. This, in turn, promotes interdepartmental engagement. Cross-training should take place at least once a month but as much as once a week. Training like this can last an entire day, or just a few hours. In order to get the best results, cross-train for at least a day at a time.

Some business leaders cross-train on a regular basis. When doing this, you may want to consider rotating employees through different trainers and departments. This will allow the employees to meet more people and learn more jobs. Watching how these training sessions play out, and who learns quickly, will give you a better idea of who should be moved up to a leadership position. This can also help identify employees that may be more productive in a different job area.

Game Days

Games are a great time to build teamwork and relieve stress. Games can be specific to teambuilding, stress relief, or any other topic. The games you should play will depend on what you want to get out of them. You may choose to host a communication building game. Maybe you want to develop a deeper sense of camaraderie. Or, maybe you just want to use game day as a creativity building exercise. No matter what game type you chose, find out what your employees would like to play and try to mix it with the style you need.

Communication building games can be as simple as the game telephone: without telling the group what you are going to say you whisper in the ear of the person next to you, they repeat the exact same thing to the person next to them, and everyone does the same around the room until the last person says it out loud. The object of this simple game is to show how communication can be distorted over a very short period of time.

A networking game might offer the chance for each person to meet everyone else. You might have them play musical partners until they have all met each other. It could be as simple as a business card collecting game. The number of creative ideas for this is endless.

The exact game is not as important as the results. Make sure you pick a game that will add something your business and people need. True leaders make almost every competitive task a friendly game.

Other teamwork building techniques may include drawing or miming games. There are also some great topics you can use for general discussion. Always encourage everyone to take part in teambuilding exercises.

Group Outings

Taking the team out for a group event is great for teambuilding. Whether you are going out to eat, to attend a seminar, or to partake in a marathon, outside events give your people experiences they can use to relate to each other. Not all employees will attend these events, but make sure you offer attendance to everyone. Spending time in the outdoors as a group is also good for the health of your team.

Taking the team out to eat is a good way to celebrate a shared victory. Accomplishments - made as a team - help solidify the teamwork mentality within your group. Don't forget to consider the budget when you are solidifying this mentality. Costs can run extremely high if you are not careful. If you need to conserve money, think about ordering pizza or something to the office.

Seminars keep you and your employees up to date on what's going on in the industry, but they usually cost more money than they claim to save you. Seminars give out large amounts of information to help your company compete in the modern business environment. They can be expensive, so you might only want to send a few employees at first. They can come back and train the rest of your people. Seminars are also great places to network with other businesses and professionals.

Bad weather might not stop indoor seminars, but it can put an immediate halt to an outside event. Still, outdoor events are a great chance to build teamwork. Egg-tossing, sack racing, and a plethora of physical sports can keep even the largest of groups satisfied all day. I like to do these events on a Friday so the participants can recuperate over the weekend. Before the big day, ask a few employees what games they would like to partake in during the teambuilding activity.

Rotating Teams

Teams can quickly develop into small clicks or groups within the company. To avoid this problem, change the teams up every event or game. Encourage people to work on a team with people they don't know. Place names in a container and pull them out one at a time to create random teams. No matter how you do it, get people working with people they don't know or haven't worked with in a while.

You may even consider getting together with another department leader to work on some events and games together.

Group Rituals

Games, events, and other things you partake in can become rituals. These are simply things people in a group share together. They connect us even when nothing else does. Some examples of rituals in the United States are: Independence Day (July, 4th), Veterans Day (November, 11), and Thanksgiving (November, 27). Society calls these rituals "holidays." In the business environment, consistent team-building and communication-building exercises everyone does together can become rituals that give the employees common ground.

Americans can be found doing very similar things on holidays. This is a memory they share with each other as a favored pastime. With common memories and pastimes to relate with, it is easier to become friends and fight for each others' common interests. Create the common interest mentality at your work with rituals and events done on a consistent basis. Be creative, there are millions of ideas to use here. Schedules and consistency are very important for solidifying rituals.

Example Schedule

There are going to be many things not included in this bare bones example schedule. This is meant to be a reference point for you to create a schedule that works for your business unit. I will give a daily schedule, a weekly schedule, a monthly schedule, and a yearly schedule. Tailor these schedules as you see fit.

Daily teambuilding and efficiency plans: (9-5 work environment)

Monday-Friday
8:45-9:15AM – Arrival to work. Get situated.
9:15-9:30AM – Meeting (Past, Present, Future)
12:00-1:00PM – Lunch
4:30PM – Teambuilding Games/Exercises
5:00PM – End of Workday

Weekly teambuilding and efficiency plans: (9-5 work environment)

Monday-Thursday
8:45-9:15AM – Arrival to work. Get situated.
9:15-9:30AM – Meeting (Past, Present, Future)
12:00-1:00PM – Lunch

5:00PM – End of Workday

Friday
8:45-9:15AM – Arrival to work. Get situated.
9:15-9:30AM – Meeting (Past, Present, Future)
12:00-1:00PM – Lunch
3:00-5:00PM – Teambuilding Games/Exercises
5:00PM – End of Workday

Monthly teambuilding and efficiency plans: (9-5 work environment)

Monday-Thursday
8:45-9:15AM – Arrival to work. Get situated.
9:15-9:30AM – Meeting (Past, Present, Future)
12:00-1:00PM – Lunch
5:00PM – End of Workday

Friday
8:45-9:15AM – Arrival to work. Get situated.
9:15-9:30AM – Meeting (Past, Present, Future)
12:00-1:00PM – Lunch
4:30PM – Teambuilding Games/Exercises
5:00PM – End of Workday

Last Friday of the Month
All day teambuilding event

Yearly teambuilding and efficiency plans:
(Any work environment)

The daily, weekly, and monthly schedule would be the same as with one of the previous plans. The main change here is the addition of a yearly action for teambuilding. These long events can be at the workplace or somewhere else. It depends on the area and environment you work in and what you most want to accomplish.

Yearly teambuilding events should be scheduled for a day to as long as a few weeks. You can have a 2-3 day event at the office, go to a park or other large congregation area for several days, or go on a prolonged work-vacation as a team. Plan the events around teamwork. You can also hire a specialist to help fill the teambuilding time.

Don't fall short on your goal of leading the curve. You have the resources at your disposal to lead your people to victory and beyond. Be the leader you have always been and go start leading the curve!

Flash Back Review

From time to time, it's a good idea to review over the things in this book. Some of them may become daily routine. Others will quickly fall from your memory. In order to be sure you are doing everything you can to improve, review this book or pick up a new one on the same subject at least once a year.

From time to time, check for updated books and consider taking a college course to refresh. Practices in management and leadership will probably never stop advancing. We need to continuously improve so we can take over and create new market share for our company. If you want to stay on top, you need to keep up to date on the latest information. Groups and events are another great way to stay up-to-date on new happenings.

Review What You Have Learned

Lead by Example:
If you want others to follow what you say, lead by example. People will not take you at your word if you break your own rules. Respect is something you can never command; it must always be earned. Leading by example is the best way to earn respect. Follow your own rules and advice.

Attitude Matters:
People will be looking at you for direction. If you have a poor attitude, they will have a poor attitude. It is your job to bring confidence to the entire organization. No matter what, you need to look like you believe everything is going to be just fine. Keep the mood in your department positive.

Time Management:

No one needs to tell a manager or leader that time management is important. Train your people to work and make decisions without you. Keep a list of things to accomplish, order them from most to least important, and do the most important first. Use a calendar or day-planner to make sure everything is done on time.

Unit Strategy Plan:

Work out an overall plan of action for your vision. Where is your company going? Write it down in detail with succession plans for your people. Go over this plan every few weeks to make sure you are still on track. You can make any necessary changes at this point.

Effective Communication:

You are going to be in big trouble if you can't communicate with your people. Effective communication is imperative to the smooth and efficient operation of any business. Individually get to know your employees. Use the language they use and keep communication open and ongoing.

Consistency:
Congratulations on your life within a fishbowl. When you make a rule, it must apply to everyone, especially you. Human beings trust consistency. Make sure your emotions don't play a role in your decisions. Consistency gives everyone something to plan against. Give your people the ability to plan ahead by working inside a system they can understand.

Networking:
Creating friends in other businesses or departments is important for when you need something. You never know when someone in another area of the business or market is going to need you and vice versa. Network with people outside of your market segment and use your network to help your employees, business, and the other people in your network connect with each other.

Mentor:
Finding a good mentor is an excellent way to build your career. You can also help build the career of someone else by doing the same when you are in a position to take on a pupil.

By helping each other we can advance in our businesses and societies much more rapidly.

Adapt with Change:
If you don't adapt with change you will become obsolete. Any market that is open to new businesses is vulnerable to market changing entrants. You must fight to stay ahead of the curve. Don't be caught off-guard by a disruptive entrepreneur who takes most of your market share. Remember that diversity helps you stay ahead of the changing curve.

Manage Stress:
It doesn't matter how great a manager you are, you can't do everything. Learn your limitations. Some things are better left to others. So, hire the right people for the job and get out of their way. If they need help, they can come to you for guidance. Use the guidance to teach them to make their own decisions. Get quality sleep and eat healthy.

Public Speaking:
Every leader has to speak in front of people from time to time. Getting the hang of public speaking techniques will help you along in

your career. Whether it's a meeting or presentation, bring a visual aid in the form of an agenda, stick with a few basic rules, and start and finish on time. Make eye contact with the group as often as possible. This will keep them attentive to your message.

Developing Teamwork:

Teamwork is imperative to a business which values efficiency, quality, and productivity. You can develop teamwork through the use of games, cross-training, and outside the office events. Teamwork development is not a "once a year" task. Building camaraderie should be a consistent process. Games can be scheduled for short daily periods, longer weekly periods, and for one day or more every month. The specifics will depend on your business.

Flash Back & Review:

It is important to review what we know every once in a while. This helps us better retain information and allows us to make sure we are doing what is best for our employees, our company, and ourselves. It is easy to get distracted and forget to do the small things.

Review a good book at least once a year to make sure you stay on track.

Leading the curve requires dedication. You have the resources to put your company on top. Consistently follow this review guide. Look back at these things after a year has passed and take note of all the positive changes.

Note to Readers

Hopefully you've enjoyed the book. If you haven't figured it out yet, I love leadership, management, and entrepreneurship. Of these, entrepreneurship is my number one passion. I believe great leaders are born to be entrepreneurs. The passion for improvement is ingrained in them.

When leaders follow the simple guidelines I've laid out here, things will improve. The total amount of improvement depends on the amount of work you are willing to put in.

I am always looking to improve my book and would love to hear from you. Please check out my website for more information about contacting me. You can easily find me on facebook, twitter, or through: www.zechariahblanchard.com.

I am available for speaking engagements and/or training sessions. Please contact me via my website for more information.

How can I make this book better? If you don't think my book is worth 5 stars I want to know why. Shoot me over an email. I would be happy to update my book to make it better. If you think it is worth 5 stars then head over to Amazon and review it now. Thanks!!!

Keep pushing the boundaries of business forward. Only by challenging the accepted can we push the envelope forward. Never give up!

Sincerely,
Zechariah Blanchard

Other books by Zechariah Blanchard
Saltwater Fish and Reef Tanks

Saltwater Fish and Reef Tanks
From Beginner to Expert

By Zechariah Blanchard

<u>Saltwater Fish and Reef Tanks</u> is a great book for the beginner saltwater hobbyist – or anyone that wants to know the easy way to own and maintain a quality saltwater reef tank.

Zechariah was the managing owner of a small saltwater aquarium store in Orlando, FL. While working in the store he helped hundreds of customers solve problems with their aquariums ranging from beginner to expert.

His book about reef aquariums is directed toward the person who wishes to learn a considerable amount of information from one location. He discusses purchase, setup, cycling, buying livestock, caring for your inhabitants, and a whole lot more!

You can find <u>Saltwater Fish and Reef Tanks</u> available in Kindle and paperback form on Amazon.com and at other major retailers. Get your copy right now!

Creativity, Innovation, and Entrepreneurship

Creativity, Innovation, and Entrepreneurship
Keys to the Future of Human Society

By Zechariah Blanchard
Copyright ©2010 Zechariah Blanchard

Creativity, Innovation, and Entrepreneurship dives into which aspects of business and society bring about the changes we love and need to move forward. Zechariah breaks down and explains creativity, innovation, and entrepreneurship in a way that is easy to understand.

He offers the reader examples and analogies to help better explain how these things play a crucial role in the future of our society.

The author believes that creativity, innovation, and entrepreneurship have played an imperative role in the past, present, and will continue to play an imperative role in the future.

Mr. Blanchard explores many different areas of creativity, innovation, and entrepreneurship. He also goes into detail about how they can be applied to individuals and groups.

Creativity, Innovation, and Entrepreneurship is available in electronic and paperback form on Amazon.com and at other major retailers. Get your copy right now!

Speaking Engagements and Seminar Training

Zechariah Blanchard is available for speaking engagements within the United States.

Mr. Blanchard can speak on any of the topics from this book or his other books.

He also offers training seminars that start at a few hours and can last as long as several days.

You can contact him about the details of a speaking engagement via his website: www.ZechariahBlanchard.com

You can also contact the author on facebook, twitter, and linkedin.

Send paper correspondence to:

Zechariah Blanchard
PO Box 677413,
Orlando, FL 32867

About the Author

 Zechariah Blanchard holds a Bachelors of Science in Business Management – Entrepreneurship from the University of Central Florida. He has worked in management at the corporate and entrepreneurial level.

Mr. Blanchard believes management and entrepreneurship are what will help usher in the future of our society. He has learned the importance of staying ahead of the curve in the business-world and enjoys passing his knowledge and passion along to other managers and leaders.

For more information about Zechariah Blanchard you can check out his website: http://www.zechariahblanchard.com

He can also be found on facebook, twitter, and by searching for him online.

Mr. Blanchard is a disruptive Entrepreneur. He graduated from the University of Central Florida with a Bachelors of Science in Business Management. Mr. Blanchard enjoys entering markets where there is room for rapid advancement and improvement on the current business climate.

Contact Zechariah at
ZJamesBlanchard@gmail.com